Cosmosis

poems and musings

Stefanie Briar
@Stefanie.briar.poetry

ISBN: 9798640249040

Instagram:

@stefanie.briar.poetry

TikTok:

@stefaniebriarpoetry

Date of Publication: 4/18/2020

First Printing: 2020

Kindle Direct Publishing

Chapter divider illustrations by Kalyani Datta

@kalyaniidatta

Cover design by Kaitlin Coppock

For Jeff;

my soul's mate,

my piece of the universe.

This little book is proof that beauty can be born

from the ashes of pain and loss.

~

Chase your dreams with a vengeance.

Time *never* waits.

When I was young,

I could never fathom

people claiming that the universe

was infinite and wide...

Until I saw it for myself

in the depths

of

your

e y e s.

 S.B. //Cosmosis

Love.

This collection is dedicated to the greatest human
experience, in all of its beauty and utter devastation.

May you lose (and find) yourself between the lines.

You've got me so high

that I'm tangled up in the clouds,

and waltzing the sky.

But when comes the rain,

and it all pours down,

I will careen head over feet;

transfixed by the sound

of my own gravity.

But as long as I'm falling in love with you,

I suspect I'll have found...

that wherever I c r a s h land

is *holy ground*.

☾ S.B. //Holy Ground

I am surely spellbound

by the stars in your eyes

that shoot down and

f

a

l

l

when you gaze into mine.

You look like the rest of my life,

and the end of "goodbye".

☾ S.B. //Spellbound

You are a warm day, and pouring rain

that I want to dance in
with utterly wild
A
            B
                    A
                        N
                            D
                                O
                                    N.

☾ **S.B. //Raindance**

Your early kisses adorn me in the light of morning.

You crown me, limbs drowning infinitely;

s

     i

       n

         k

           i

             n

               g

                 ...

neatly into you.

☾ S.B. //Neatly Into You

It's a curious concept;
"Home" is usually a place...

a space to belong
where life makes sense;
a respite, a comfort.

It is the sigh at the end of a long day;
a place to stem the flow of hurting...

but sometimes, we find that
"Home" is a   p e r s o n.

☾ **S.B. //Hom e**

I want to say that we are more

than just the sum of our parts,

but here we are:

One love.

Two twin souls.

Three tries.

Four light eyes...

just trying to

get

     it

         right.

☾ **S.B. //Love by Numbers**

It doesn't matter what we're doing;
I would spend every single moment
of my life and time
doing nothing or *anything*
with you.

It would all be worth it and well spent
in the end,

as long as I have you
to come

H
O
M
E

to.

☾ S.B.//Nothing or Anything

In my love for you,
I birthed the moon.
I kissed suns,
I

h
    u
       n
          g

                galaxies,
and I stirred stars
from a shaker of the salt of the earth;
acre by acre; tending *us*.

       I spoke worlds of your eyes,
and of the strands of bluegrass shoots inside.

With each b r u s h
of your hand on mine
Spring feels imminent, and poems rhyme.

New life g r o w s
from each pore of my seeded surface;
wildflower meadows chasing the spent earth...
remade new; whole
with a rain-soaked silk tourniquet
stemming the hurt.

We're a yellow-bruised "perfect"...
when fought for; worth it.

Suspended together,
we are divinely tethered
to tilled fields within us:

Two; but *one*.

☾ **S.B.//Eternal Spring**

Our eyes meet,

and our mouths aren't moving,

but make no mistake...

we are still speaking, and dreaming,

and believing in us,

and

f

a

l

l

i

n

g

in love.

☾ **S.B. //The Eyes Have It**

Falling in love is a process;

frozen in motion, like falling asleep...

you can't see it happening.

 It occurs slowly,

 over a rippled interval,

and then...all at once,

the

 f

 a

 l

 l

 i

 n

 g.

Not like skinned knees and scrapes;

 like every single piece fallen into place.

☾ **S.B. //You've Fallen**

I am addicted

to the lines in your skin,

the light in your eyes,

and the fire in your touch.

I can never get   e n o u g h.

I'd

i n j e c t

you into my veins,

inhale you straight into my brain,

revel in the haze and let the world fade away.

If I should overdose of this affliction,

do not revive me of my condition.

I'd gladly die like this,

                    and then be   r e b o r n   upon your lips.

☾ **S.B. //Addict**

I stand across from you, my mirror,

and in the depths of your eyes

I finally see clearly...

I love you with all I have,

and you reflect the same love right back.

We see the *truth* without trying to,

and here you are in front of me;

a reflection of all p o s s i b i l i t y.

Come what may,

there will never come a day

where I can look away from **you.**

☾ **S.B. //My Mirror**

Lazy weekend mornings,

sun filtering urgent light beams

through drifting curtains.

My alarm clock is the warmth of you.

The scent of your skin, the taste of it,

the breath gently shared and taken;

we are at one with the dawn in sacred intimacy.

I will chase your soul,

early

and

y e l l o w,

like the sunrise...

all the days of my life.

☾ **S.B. //Sunrise**

In all sights I have seen,

in all words I have spoken,

I've never experienced the emotion

that overtakes me when you look my way.

Under the ocean of your eyes,

I cannot

h

i

d

e

a n y t h i n g.

Here we are, as old as stars;

speaking sighs like lullabies.

☾ **S.B. //Sighs and Lullabies**

I've always felt invisible,

painfully ordinary,

run-of-the-mill,

(nothing special about me).

Yet you always look at me

like *I'm all you see.*

All at once, I am transformed,

and not to be ignored...

and *extraordinary*.

☾ **S.B //Extraordinary**

From the starting line
you and I
were   w i l d   growing things;

like ivy vines chasing the sky,
then tangling like

                        w

                    e

                        e

                            d

                                s.

☾ S.B. //Wild Growing Things

I love the way our gazes meet

and we speak silently;

our own language,

born of a long history,

and of the time spent

knowing one another completely.

A comfort unlike any other

lives in how we "fit" together.

We are the perfect pair of jeans,

worn in *just right* at the

   s

      e

 a

     m

 s.

   ☾ **S.B. //Fit Together**

My open book,

you wear your words, written but unheard

on your sleeve, unable to pretend to me.

The pages

F

A

L

L

open,

all the way to the ending,

and I read you

like the words stuck on the tip of my tongue.

When I drag my finger, light as a feather

along the length of your spine,

you *shiver* along the seams

of your tight bindings.

They will loosen in time,

but for me *only*.

☾ **S.B. //My Open Book**

I am still not sure

how you permeated my shell

and worked your way in underneath my skin.

I am usually so careful

to keep the world out,

       but with you

I was exposed from the beginning.

Now I don't know where exactly you begin

and I

               e   d.

                     n

☾ **S.B. //Permeation**

Worlds collide when your hand brushes mine,

and in us resides

the   magic   that   h-i-d-e-s

inside the tips of our fingers.

It fans out in melodic timbres,

singing the song

of how it feels to be One with someone.

☾ S.B. //To Be One

Your intoxicating magic,
like ink blots on fingertips,
spills out all over my skin
and sinks in beneath it
as I sink deeper into you.

I breathe you in,
and welcome the end
of my beginning.

Transform me;
transfix me,
bewitch me with your alchemy.

Make me something new
and whole, and beautiful;

☾ **S.B. //Alchemy**

Like a rainbow of filtered light

in unexpected places,

yours is the magic I'm always craving

between the spaces of our heartbeats.

You are the light in

                       e

                  v

              e

           r

        y

t

   h

     i

       n

        g

☾ S.B. //Prismatic

You are the tide; ever-changing, vacillating, undulating.

You change your mind and reasons;

you ebb and flow with the days and seasons,

and you retreat when things get difficult.

You "avoid" backwards, back into yourself.

I don't think it has ever dawned on you that I am your moon;

your constant that you can always count upon to move you.

We have always moved this cosmic way,

The only difference now is that

our awareness of one another has been awakened.

We were created to work as one; we exist to affect one another.

No amount of your surging or retreating could release this hold.

You and I, tide and moon, are as old as stardust.

We are comprised of the same universal matter;

designed in tandem, made for one another.

☾ **S.B. //Tide And Moon**

At the end of my life

when my soul takes flight,

I will hang on for dear life

to the nearest living thing...

dying to go back and love you

      all

             over

                  again.

☾ **S.B. //All Over Again**

I cannot even look at you
without bursting into flames.

I am dying to hear my name upon your lips
as I devour every inch of you.

I am hungry;
so hungry.

I hope you'll feed me.

☾ **S.B. // Need**

I don't believe in God,

but I invoke him, and I moan for him,

and I scream his holy name

when you are here with me in this bed;

skin on skin, hands in hair...

a devil's stare that is h e a v e n sent.

No force of nature could ruin this holy communion...

The altar is free,

and so inviting.

I've been *on my knees* a while now;

his name is still the one on my lips

as my body

             d

                  i

                         p

                                s,

and hands rock my hips

until the moon dissolves into light of day.

So let me bow my head, arch my back,

bite my lower lip, throw my hair back...

          and p r a y.

☾ **S.B. //Name In Vain**

It has occurred to me

that I would do *anything* you say

if we are in bed

and your hands are busy...

☾ **S.B. //Submission**

I revel in learning your topography;
a map leading me to *ecstasy,*
deliciously lost in your majestic peaks
and undulating valleys, sloping

      d

          o

               w

                    n

and surrounding me.

Around each new corner,
I will be your explorer.

I love every line in your skin
enough to ignore this

          m   e   s   s
       we're in.

☾ S.B. //Explorer

I come before you,

ripe for consumption.

I am waiting,

open,

and so ready

for you to ruin me.

☾ **S.B. //Ruin**

There are fragments of me;

twisted, knotted nooks and crannies

that are wild, untamed, overgrown,

unexplored, and vastly ignored.

I want you to *crash through me* with a machete,

and turn over every grain of earth,

wrangle every climbing weed;

tame the wild inside of me...

(but not completely).

☾ **S.B. //Wild**

I never need to be empowered,

I only crave to be devoured;

disembodied from my own limbs

to sink or swim with you

in the rolling sea of this bed…

panting; floating; wet; spent,

in surrendered submission.

You can all but own me,

as long as you promise

to keep your hands busy

and your mouth wandering.

Write your name on my skin,

brand me with your fingerprints.

Be sure to leave your mark

when you take what's yours;

(I want to see it in the morning).

I worship upon the altar of you;

I paid my tithes and I want my due.

So whisper in my ear, and tell me exactly

what you want me to *do*.

☾ **S.B. //Tell Me What to Do**

The things you do to me

are dark,

enticing,

terrifying,

menacing:

you have overwritten and rewired me.

Your skin on mine...

it makes me sing,

makes me scream,

brings me to life again.

Conquer me,

cage me,

keep me in chains,

as long as

you never stop

s i g h i n g my name.

☾ S.B. //The Things You Do

Isn't it strange?

One look in your eyes fans the flames,

and I'm burning, and melting inside,

and deranged with desire.

I am crazy for you,

and you're mad for me, too.

Let's devour this madness

that both fuels and

c o n s u m e s.

☾ **S.B. //Fuel the Fire**

Black Hole

Implosion, erosion, time in slow motion;

    you chewed up and spat out my unwanted devotion

    like words that never tasted right on your tongue.

I *drown* in color as you fill my lungs with promises.

I black out as you break them...

    I will not

surface

    again.

☾ **S.B. //It's Over**

For all of my wandering,

for all the restlessness in my feet,

for all of my mindless meandering...

I was led to you.

We collided unexpectedly,

intertwined beautifully, and

after stargazing in your eyes once,

I knew I would never again wish for daylight

or curse the night.

I tore up the map designed to take me onward,

Dug in my heels and my heart,

and set up camp beside you;

not caring where we'd go, as long as I never lost those stars

or strayed too far from those arms.

Now, tears are ink blots dotting our story's annihilating end:

The stars are gone, and

I can't even see the sky anymore.

I pace vacant halls in a house of locked doors

serving the life sentence you've handed me;

the end

of stargazing.

☾ **S.B. //Stargazing**

Once greater,

now the unwelcome spectator,

I'll view your life in pictures...

watch you live behind a screen;

puzzle piece scenes, with no place for me.

I'm headsick with a heartbleed

and I'd rather watch you

     b

        r

          e

             a

               t

                 h

                   e.

☾ S.B. //Spectator

The air is dry; stale.

The halls are still and empty;

the floors are cold against my feet.

The silence of you and me screams,

and ricochets back into me.

Where once you filled me with golden light,

now there lives an endless night;

a heart that's grown weary, too resigned to fight.

You're still a sight for a sore mind,

but you're not mine tonight.

We can't repeat the past;

can't get it back.

The curtain call has faded black

as we breathe our last.

With the staying power of every promise I ever made,

and every dream that you will never make come true...

Unbroken but bruised;

I *release* you.

☾ **S.B. //I Release You**

You impacted my life with a shot in the dark,

and a break to the heart.

I played your perfect, little fool;

trying desperately to keep you.

We die a miniscule but definite death

when we are cast aside and left

for a future we are uninvited to:

No dagger pierces like the t r u t h.

I still wear the knife you placed in my back

like a badge of honor...

you have a knack for slaying me.

☽

☾ **S.B. //Slayed**

You want to hold me hostage

in a dungeon on the outside;

starve me of you until I've gone quiet,

wall off the memory of me,

and keep me somewhere out of sight...

But I still haunt you in the deep of night;

   I am closest to your mind when you close your eyes.

It is the hostage who ultimately escapes,

and the *haunted* who is driven mad with pain.

☾ S.B. //The Hostage

When you are a someone
desirous of being another someone's everything,
you are bound to be returned from whence you came.

When you want the world;
the sun, the moon, their galaxies,
and their stars exploding into supernovas...

you will be lucky to be left with sand particles;
stardust to slip through the cracks of your fingers.
Your intentions will eclipse you.

The conundrum belies that the one who wants all
is the one left with none;
the obsessor craves to be the sole possessor
and is rendered the lesser in the end.

Find the *one piece* of them that you can call your own,
and content yourself to call it "home".

☾ **S.B. //Part and Parcel**

Today,

as the sunlight started to break,

as soon as I began to wake,

I lingered halfway between dreams and reality;

lost in the in-between,

where you are still mine

and everything will be

a l l

       r i g h t.

☾ S.B. //Halfway Between Dreams

Imagine my devastation

when I realized you had been writing fiction

while I had been penning our memoir...

Two narrators;

worlds

a   p   a   r   t.

☾ S.B. //Genre Dysphoria

In the book of us,

we wrote at your pace;

I was only the margins holding your place

while *y o u* dictated the page.

I wanted to help set the narrative,

but you decided *everything*

by choosing n o t h i n g.

You stopped our story

in the middle   of a sentence,

and I haven't heard from you since.

☾ **S.B. //Wordplayed**

When you meet him,

and the conversation flows like water,

and you can't drink him in fast enough

 to quench your thirst,

just remember, he first was mine.

And it's *me* he'll picture when he's *inside* of you

and   c l o s e s   his eyes.

☾ **S.B. //Possessive**

Your indentation

in the bed next to me

will linger long after you

l

e

a

v

e.

☾ S.B. //Indentation

Thorns and underbrush

encroach the road that leads back to us.

You are not the type to clear the path,

and I am not desperate enough to beg you back.

You owe it to me to break the silence,

but you will instead let saplings become trees

b e t w e e n   us.

Hope can't overtake a live oak.

☾ **S.B. //Between Us**

You;

my drug of choice,

my kind of high;

You hit my veins and I

F L Y.

Swim through my bloodstream

until you are *made of me*.

W   a   i   t...

NO.

I don't want you.

<u>I don't need you</u>.

Let this haze be just a dream...

In the morning I'll be clean,

I just need *to feel something*.

This is my last hit,

I promise it.

So lace it with regret,

and make it   q u i c k .

☾ **S.B. //Last Hit**

Wearing my best accelerant

while you stood, complicit,

I lit myself ablaze,

and I raged for you.

Instead of dousing the flames,

you pulled up a chair

and used me to keep warm;

you sat and watched me burn.

You're still picking through my ashes

looking for embers...

I hope you

C   E

H   K

O

on the smoke.

☾ S.B. //Smoke Signal

I picture us an hourglass:

It's just released
Its final grain of sand.

I just want to turn it over
and start again,

but I can't.

☾ **S.B. //Hourglass**

I let you break my eggshell heart,
and scramble the yolk of my yellow soul.

I'm now an unrecognizable mess,
and you're just sitting there calmly eating breakfast.

☾ **S.B. //Sunday Side Up**

Ever since you pulled the rug
out from under my blindsided feet,
I tiptoe through life...

waiting for people to leave.

☾ **S.B. //Tiptoe**

The air is alive with tendrils of tension;

swirling and

c   g

  u   n

    r   i

      l

around the "us" shaped space

that gravity fails to make heads or tails of

when we actively try not to embrace,

and instead pretend we were glad to part ways.

Instead, there is replacement

somewhere adjacent to false appraisement

of each hand concealed; never to be played.

We will lay our cards (and stars) to rest,

and then

leave

      them

          that

              way.

Finally,

we will give up and walk away,

before either of us breaks and begs the other to stay.

"It was so good seeing you again;

have a nice day."

☾ S.B. // Missed Connection

Stop this madness;

turn around, this isn't right.

You are meant to be in my life.

I know it.

I feel it.

I breathe it.

I see it.

The stars planned on us,

so how can I give up?

☾ **S.B. //Against the Stars**

I've planted the seeds of our motionless story,
and I've watered them with salt, bittersweetly.

I watch them grow;
harvested and devoured off the tangled vine,
by people online who we'll
never

    even

      know.

☾ S.B. //Dead Stories Have No Glory

Years down the line,

at an undetermined point in time,

when I am looking back on the experiences of my life,

the splendid; the sublime,

and those marked by cold regret...

I'd stake my life on it that

the story I lived with you will always s c r e a m   the loudest.

It will *bleed* off the pages.

It will roll off my tongue

like *slow honey;*

golden and glowing,

taking cover in color...

still refusing to be over.

☾ **S.B. //The Screaming Story**

Before you,

I never knew

you could still B   U   R   N   for someone

while standing *in their rain*,

and still love someone

who is the one who caused the pain.

☾ **S.B. //Burning in the Rain**

"Home" is a place I no longer recognize;

these eyes, once full of sunlight,

can no longer distill the sun in the sky

from the horizon line, which, at our sunrise,

held worlds; held everything.

It used to bring and hold so much magic,

and promise, and possibility.

I used to want to walk it like a tightrope;

the thin stretch of life would be ours alone.

I'd build our home where dreams can't die...

we'd kiss the stars

and

      one

           another

                g o o d n i g h t.

But now,

home is only the skin I am stitched into,

not the dreams I longed to cling to.

So I will sit here, resolute,

and stare into the horizon line

until our sunset becomes a *sunrise*.

S.B. //Dead Horizon

It will kill you

to see the love you once worshipped

breathing laboriously; on life support...

hooked up to what it once was

(which will never be enough to save it).

You go to pull the plug,

but it's *you*

who comes   u n   d   o   n e.

☾ **S.B. //Life Support**

Your red flags and stagnation

give me   -w-h-i-p-l-a-s-h-,

so here's my white flag and resignation

before my neck can   —s-n-a-p-.

☾ S.B. //Red Flags

When a h e a r t b e a t away is the greatest distance

between two objects, now broken down,

the two together become a living clock tower:

a death knell without a sound.

The two hands, hours and seconds,

are locked in a tandem dance,

and will only cross one another's paths for a moment,

before moving away again.

They're a constant m*issed connection.*

☾ S.B. //Clock Tower

I erected cities to you
with adoration on my tongue,
and you burnt mine to the ground
in the wake of your "love".

☾ **S.B. //Cities**

Ever since you came

and wrote your name inside every tear I cry

(a signature to remember you by),

the skin pulled tight over my face

is a wasteland;

where waiting is choked with ligatures of hope,

where magic and myth and the echoes of love

all

      go

          to

               die.

Every memory that falls starts out fluid and warm,

but reaches my lips half-dried and

          c   d.

             o   l

☾ **S.B. //Saving Face**

I am here, haunted but hopeful

that we will grow back together again in the end.

So I send you what is left of my heart

as I start to let you go;

until then.

☾ S.B. //As I Start To Let You Go

The bed can be an ocean,

the space between sheets; a shipwreck,

flanked by floating debris...

the

                                                    s

                                        i

                            n

                    k

                    i

                            n

                                    g

death of you and me.

☾ S.B. //Shipwreck

Like a stained dress,

it's useless;

I cannot wash you out of me.

In every fiber of my being,

in every nucleus in my every cell,

in every live wire of a nerve ending,

your every molecule is fused with me.

Every song in my soul is tuned to you like an instrument.

The *stain* of you *seeps* through me,

and alters my essential chemistry.

☾ **S.B. //The Stain**

Stillness, silence;

nothing left of you and me...

this isn't what's supposed to be.

Bitterness, loneliness;

every face in a crowded room,

every hope that fades to gloom...

is y o u.

☾ **S.B. //Stillness, Silence**

I have killed you, killed us

so many times on paper.

Each time,

you just get up and dust yourself off:

"Let's try this again later."

☾ **S.B. //Kill Your Darling**

How will I ever remember to breathe,

when you have stolen my lungs from me?

That's what it feels like...

that you have taken my life from me.

My heart barely beats.

My eyes see nothing but your memory.

How long?

How long until I return to normalcy,

until I come back to <u>me</u>?

☾ S.B. // Stolen

You are so loud,

and live in countless sounds.

You are banging drums;

a bass that thrums with thumping heat

that alters the rhythm of my heartbeat.

You are sirens wailing,

blasting and tailing

too

      close

          behind

             me.

You are every turned-up song that

d

r

i

v

e

s me home,

every lyric that we once sang along

(or made love) to.

Bells ring, heralding every thought of you

in siren calls that

s

   t

i

   r

my blood anew.

And after a busy day of the noise of you,

you're the quiet

d

r

i

p

of water like tears

from a faucet, too.

☾ S.B. //Noise of You

You'd have come back if you were willing,

but you never did,

and my love is owed more than passive resistance.

So I got up,

excused myself from the table

where respect and love were no longer served

and had grown   c o l d.

It's time I got what I *deserve.*

☾ **S.B. //Just Desserts**

If I could have collected

every tear shed that had your name on it,

by now,

I'd have an ocean that I could

d

     r

        o

           w

              n

in,

and *forget*.

☾ S.B. //Raw Salt

I bloomed when I met you,

now I've wilted; dried; died; been lied to,

pressed between the closed pages

of a story I once believed could shake the earth.

So consume me, entomb me, exhume me;

use me up again until I'm spent,

then turn me back to ash.

It wouldn't be the first time,

and I doubt it's the last.

☾ **S.B. //Spent Cinders**

I touch you in all the wrong places,

in all the right ways.

You beg me to stay,

but that is not the kind of game I play.

☾ **S.B. //Chess not Checkers**

Hope waits,

a left-on porch light, glowing, watching:

a silent sentinel

waiting on guard to guide you home.

Hope dances

like dropped bombs raining from the sky.

I sidestep the shrapnel that kisses my skin,

finding a home in it.

Hope is a bird that sings and sings,

and sings;

lullabies (or dirges)

for a love that won't give in.

☾ S.B. //Waiting on Tenterhopes

Oh, you're posting passive aggressive lyrics?
Of course, love, that's the spirit.

Why directly *speak* to me
when you can do it vaguely and lazily
with someone else's lines and poetry?

Am I not worth a bit of creativity?
This is really getting *boring*.

☾ **S.B. //Passive Aggressive Obsessive**

You and I exist in oil-spill rainbows,

questions loom like shades of grey.

We spin like tops, roulette shots,

which chamber of our hearts

will we empty out today?

Dissected within an inch of life,

frozen hearts in formaldehyde,

we tempt fate by measured degrees.

We sharpen blades to hit cleanly.

We push our buttons; press our luck.

We turn on a dime; timed like a stopwatch

somewhere left of the center...

a game we claim we dare not enter.

Where's the prize if we see the end?

Doesn't somebody have to win?

So problematic, so calculated

so cruel and complicated.

Hearts are not a game to hack.

I open my palm; a white flag,

"Can I have mine back?"

☾ **S.B. //Not A Game**

I envy the constant moon

and every ancient star

for being able to watch over you always...

while I am here;

F

      A

          R

from both your stars and your heart.

☾ S.B. //Faraway

I'm somehow closest to your mind
when you *close your eyes*.

Even in the dark, I can see
that all of your demons
are shaped like *m e*.

☾ **S.B. //Dem ons**

When you said you weren't going anywhere,

that you'd be there always,

what you meant was "until it fades".

And in the morning,

you were gone without a   t   r   a   c   e.

☾ **S.B. //Until it Fades**

You are the poem

I don't know how to write.

Normally,

I manipulate words like marionette strings.

I make them dance and sing so effortlessly.

But with you; for you?

They dress in armor, a storied stampede,

and fight me on most everything.

They toss and turn,

they hiss and burn,

and I've yet to learn

how to make them come out right.

The one damned thing

I'm supposed to be able to do

is

w

      r

          i

              t

                e.

I fear I will die

with a poem for you still screaming in my mouth,

clamoring to burst out...

and there will be _nothing_ I can do about it.

☾ **S.B. //The Poem I Can't Write**

This broken heart

in all its shards of magnificence

are a testament; a treasured mosaic

of everything broken that was once a dream

back in the days of

Y

O

U

&

M

E.

☾ **S.B. //Mosaic heart**

If ever one day you sit and ruminate,

carefully contemplate the agonizing choice...

"To stay, or to go?"

I'd rather you go.

I only need the kind of love

that **knows** it belongs in my tomorrows.

☾ S.B. //In My Tomorrows

Neither of us

is who the other really wants,

but we smile and shrug,

and jump into bed just the same.

I'll help you forget her

if you ignore it

when I call you by *his* name.

☾ S.B. //The Kindness of Strangers

Two paper airplanes take flight;
light and free.

In the end, they're brought down
by the very sky they craved:

but pouring rain tends to disintegrate...
and they could

n

       o

             t

be saved.

☾ S.B. //Paper Airplanes

Two fingers are locked and loaded
around and through handles shining.
The blade is waiting; open.

I gaze steadily down
at the invisible cord that connects us.
Does it know I'm here?
Can it feel the end is near?

Eyes squeezed closed
(I can't watch this happen),
there's a metallic sound, a cord severed;
the deed irrevocable.

What have I done?

Did I need more time to think it over?
What if things
had
      gotten
         better?

Our lifeline cut like an artery,

I bleed out and fall to the ground.

I always knew you would be

the

       d e a t h

               of

                   me.

☽ **S.B. //Cut the Cord**

The long-awaited paradox

greets me like a ticking clock:

as I become more sure that you are never coming back,

I let you fade into more of a blur, which I could never do before.

Is this acceptance?

Is this what "hopeless" is?

Isn't it what they said would happen?

I once lived for the pressure of your kiss,

but now I fear I am beginning to forget it.

Photographs stored away in my heart,

memories preserved like shine from stars

that I longed to cling to,

force me to open shaking hands,

trying to filter diamonds from sand,

and then return them to the ocean where I think they belong.

So why does letting go feel so wrong?

Here goes nothing…

I dive in and drown like I used to in the deep blue of your eyes,

waves rolling and breaking, the current drifting me far and wide.

I feel resolute, but my hands shake, and my heart is breaking.

Float me out; let me weep.

Let the clouds in the sky rain over me.

Let the horizon sing me to sleep.

I wish you wanted to be mine to keep,

but you are as gone as the ghost that clings on beside me

as "we" are swallowed in the sea.

☾ S.B. //Swallowed in the Sea

Dreams are the only way that I can resurrect us,

the otherworldly experience that we were;

divine when combined.

When I crave you so badly that my insides ache,

and the fire that we were burns the bitterness away,

I

      come

            to

                find

                    you

                        and

                            e s c a p e.

Dancing behind my eyes is a world in blurs,

where your lies and my tears

n

     e

        v

           e

             r   were.

We were manic.

We were magic.

We were beautiful,

and tragic,

and more than any dream could hold.

I wake; shaken.

The room is

       c

               o

                         l

                                 d.

☾ **S.B. //Dreamscape**

I used to never fear the winter cold,

I was fine with ice and the

c

r

u

n

c

h

of snow,

under white boots that took me back to childhood innocence.

I'd

      fling

            myself

                backwards,

                landing in puffs of powder,

a trust exercise between me and the weather.

Now the bitter cold makes me feel about a thousand years old,

because it parallels the fact that my heart is frozen,

and you're no longer open to a life that holds a place for me.

So, forget the winter.

Forget the bitter.

Forget the cold...

and the snow,

and absolutely everything

that doesn't include *you*.

☾ **S.B. //Love in Winter**

You should use caution when causing the exhaustion

that sets in when you use a good woman

until she is fully spent down to the last drop;

the final morsel of her love that she saved for you

and you quickly used up.

Once you have finished with her,

and she is as good as gone,

you'll wonder... without *her*, how will you go on?

You will go to her; apologize.

She will look you dead in the eyes,

and tell you she has been waiting so unbearably long

to hear you say those words.

But now that she has,

they are the most ***worthless*** she has ever heard.

☾ **S.B. //Last Drop**

There are no lies in my fire,

but right now I am too tired

to burn for you anymore...

unless *you* are the one

to stoke the

f

l

a

m

e

s

once more.

☾ **S.B. //Burnout**

I keep fighting fate with quills in a quiver,

and pages for armor.

I am writing against it, yet I'm somehow defenseless;

pressing fading bruises,

new blood in old wounds.

There's no gain or glory, but here I am still; coaxing our story

out of the hemispheres and the "never-clear"

of my train window brain...

which has tried (in vain) through the fog and the grey

to back out and black out over and over again..

desperate to escape the pain of *your* escape.

☾ **S.B. //Escape Your Escape**

There is much to be said

about the walking dead that's left of me;

stumbling around, duty-bound.

I am feeding off the words you said,

and the forgotten flesh once laid in bed

as we pressed our hopes together,

and got out of our heads,

and spoke with our hearts instead.

Now I wander this world,

wanting only to feed

upon the discarded scraps

of our broken dreams.

☾ S.B. //Walking Dead

Silver, glowing, like mercury rising,

you washed over me in waves of metallic chrome

that lit me up and felt like home.

In the moment, nothing seemed to be wrong;

like puzzle pieces falling into place,

with easy grace, we belonged.

But the realization set in slowly,

and then all at once when you were gone...

you were p o i s o n   all along.

☾ S.B. //Mercury Rising

I give our story freely, openly,

and routinely back to the world...

because, for all the world,

I wanted to give my heart *to you*,

but you refused to take it from me.

So I instead give it to them,

through poetry.

☾ **S.B. //Transfer of Energy**

It's interesting (if a little sad)
that I look for you everywhere I am,
and everywhere I go.

...I know...

You wanted to be free;
to clean your life of the stain of me.

But I can't help that I can't help that I miss you,
and I wish you would just appear out of thin air,
anywhere and everywhere.

☾ **S.B. //Everywhere**

I am brave yet broken,
introverted yet outspoken,
and so many other qualities
that you never appreciated.

Someone will someday.

☾ **S.B. //Someday**

You are the moon;

I gaze up but cannot touch you.

You pull me in like the tide,

but I can't reach you from the other side.

Oh, how I have howled in desperate desperation...

you will never be

close

        to

             me.

☾ S.B. //My Moon

Your hands,

invisibly intense around my neck,

are a gentle vice grip, squeezing life out of and into me.

My breathing slows,

and goes from gulps to shallows,

as my life with you flashes before my eyes.

So before they forever close,

put your lips on mine

o n e

    l a s t

        t i m e.

I will open them to you loving me again.

☾ **S.B. //This is the End**

I would always choose to be hurt by your words
rather than your silence.

Words may exaggerate pain,
but silence   a n n i h i l a t e s.

☾ **S.B. //The Sword of Silence**

I am wandering the earth

walking in circles towards you,

and I am only

l

o

s

t

because you are not looking for me.

☾ S.B. //Wanderlost

This is why you can't have nice things (like *me*);

because you break literally everything.

So keep on spinning pure gold into shit,

and then trying to avoid

s   t

       e   p

             p   i

                    n   g

in it.

(Good luck with that).

☾ **S.B. //The Wrecker**

I can't remember your scent,

fading like stadium lights over my waiting hope,

as I stand alone at the end of a road

you turned off of a long time ago.

I knew it would come to this,

but I ignored it because I miss you.

The clouds part, the skies open,

and the deluge begins.

Surprisingly, instead of "rained on",

I am washed clean of you, and it's over.

I go home alone,

and it doesn't feel so lonely anymore.

☾ **S.B. //After the Rain**

Together, like claps of thunder rumbling the world,

we made the perfect storm; volatile, and alive in every form.

We made grey look like rainbows,

and torn pages look like prose.

Which is why it's now so gutting and loud

to be drowning without you in the drought.

☾ **S.B. //The Perfect Scorn**

The crumpled dress in the back of my closet

that I last made love to you in

smells of you, and my perfume

and nostalgia, and regret.

I want to water it with my tears;

see if we grow back.

Instead, I rip it to shreds,

and burn it.

☾ **S.B. //The Dress**

Thank you for leaving and lying to me;
you gave me endless poetry.

If you had stayed, and the pen had stilled,
where on earth would I be now?

You stole my heart,
but I kept the words...
and I will keep spilling them out one by one,
until every last

p

i

e

c

e

of you is gone.

☾ **S.B. //I Kept the Words**

In between the moments like labor pains,

when missing you shallows my breathing,

I'm able to hold on to grounding thoughts of our better days.

I recall the fire in your kiss,

the strands of starlight hung in your eyes,

and the countless reasons why we always felt like home.

And when I can feel the next swells of pain coming,

with gritted teeth and white knuckles,

I breathe through them, and lean into them.

I gaze through the window of my mind's eye,

holding fast to the nostalgia that I remember you by.

I *so* loved when you were mine,

and I hope you think of me too, sometimes.

☾ **S.B. //Hereafter**

Now that we are done,

and our story's reached its end,

I won't let you think you've won

by allowing bitterness to win.

Once upon a moment,

I loved you like air to breathe.

I'd have all but let you own my love,

but you wouldn't stay with me.

Can't stoke a fire with regret,

or hang stars in a falling sky.

Nothing blooms in broken promises

where spent love goes to die.

In the quiet space left behind

after your blazing trail of smoke,

I refuse to be cold and unkind

though I've lost my faith in you.

You never meant a word you said,

though I meant every one of mine.

I hung on tight until the end,

and you will fade in time.

I may not be okay right now, but someday I'll be *fine*.

☾ **S.B. //After the End**

Today,

as the light breaks,

I wake; eyes open

for the first time in a long time.

And I can't help but think that

today is a good day to return home to myself.

With that thought, I smile; strange...

(it's been a while).

It's time to rise and shine,

to remove the layers of dust that built up

in the wake of the days when you were mine.

I pass the mirror,

and I stare into the eyes of a stranger.

It's time she and I got acquainted.

Over coffee and stories that she stored in a pen,

through ink tears on paper, she comes home again,

and

       draws

           the

               curtains.

A beat.

A breath.

A deep sigh.

She lets in the sunlight,
and gazes out the window at the *rest of her life*.

☾ **S.B. //Homecoming**

I   b l o o m

from the spot

where I pulled you out of me by the roots,

wishing I did not have to choose

between my sanity and an open wound.

But the rain has come and closed me up.

Now, I have room to

G   R   O   W.

☾ S.B. //Moving On

Thank you for reading this journey through the universe of love.

If you're happy, may you remain content.

If your heart is broken, may the pieces mend.

If you've come out the other side and returned to yourself...happy *homecoming!*

I wish you the kind of love that we all long for.

Love always,

S.B.

About the Author

Stefanie Briar is a wife, mother, English teacher, poet, and editor from New Jersey.

Stefanie holds bachelor's degrees in English and Secondary Education, as well as a minor in psychology. She has taught reading and writing since 2008, and became a writer in the fall of 2019, at the age of 34. She started her Instagram page (and sharing her writing) in January of 2020, and she has not looked back since.

She can be found on Instagram @stefanie.briar.poetry

and on TikTok @stefaniebriarpoetry.

Other books by Stefanie Briar:

Homecoming

Burn

Printed in Great Britain
by Amazon

80805902R10072